1 –
6/22

VOICES OF SAN FRANCISCO

Speaking Out from the City by the Bay

Edited by
Antoinette May
&
Vernon Appleby

HarperCollins*West*
A Division of HarperCollins*Publishers*

Illustrations: © 1994 Philip Burke

Front cover illustrations:
Top row: Joe Montana, Joan Baez
Middle row: Willie Mays, Amy Tan,
            Jack London, Cecil Williams
Bottom row: Dianne Feinstein, Robin Williams,
            Johnny Mathis

Back cover: Barnaby Conrad

Inside front cover flap: Cecil Williams

Inside back cover flap: Jerry Brown

VOICES OF SAN FRANCISCO: *Speaking Out from the City by the Bay*. Copyright © 1994 by HarperCollins Publishers. All rights reserved. Printed in the United States of America. No part of this book may be used or reproduced in any manner whatsoever without written permission, except in the case of brief quotations embodied in critical articles and reviews. For information, address HarperCollins Publishers, 10 East 53rd Street, New York, NY 10022.

FIRST EDITION

Library of Congress Cataloging-in-Publication Data:

May, Antoinette.
  Voices of San Francisco : speaking out from the city by
the bay / Antoinette May.
    p.   cm.
  ISBN 0-06-258654-8
  1. San Francisco (Calif.)—Quotations, maxims, etc.
  2. Celebrities—California—San Francisco—Quotations.
I. Title.
F869.S34M39 1994
979.4'61—dc20   94-12828
                                                 CIP

95 96 97 98 ❖ HAD 10 9 8 7 6 5 4 3 2

This edition is printed on acid-free paper that meets the
American National Standards Institute Z39.48 Standard

Contents

When the Franciscan fathers and their company arrived on the fateful September day in 1776, the only inhabitants of the tawny sandhills had been a handful of Indians in a *rancheria* at the corner of what is now Beach and Hyde streets. The rest was wild landscape and wild animals—the gorgeous Bay, the undulating line of the seven hills waiting for their burden of a western Rome, the windblown color-of-gold sands, chaparral, wild currant and gooseberry and rosebushes, hawthorn, a few stunted evergreen oaks, the Indian-bodied manzanita, down toward the Bay an especially extensive patch of the fragrant herb which was to give its Yerba Buena name to the cove settlement, and scattered lagoons and marshes edged with watercress and white with the stirring wings of thousands of geese, cranes, egrets, pelicans, and gulls.

Julia Altrocchi, historian

CHAPTER 1

Early Days to Love Days

~~~~~~~

Lucius Beebe
Writer, historian, and bon vivant

San Francisco, since the earliest years of the American occupancy, has always been a money town. When John Jacob Astor was clipping dimes in the trade in New York real estate and Commodore Vanderbilt was ferrying passengers to Staten Island for a shilling, the wife of San Francisco's Mayor William K. Garrison was pouring tea from a solid gold service, the first such in America, and J. W. Tucker, the town's first jeweler, was advertising silver watches that weighed a full honest pound, since no miner could be found who would carry one that weighed less.

Hubert Howe Bancroft
Early historian

Woman played her part in early California . . .
by reason of her absence.

~~~

Black Bart
Notorious San Francisco bandit of the 1870s,
left this poem in a strongbox after he'd robbed it

I've labored long and hard for bread,
For honor and for riches,
But on my corns too long you've tread,
You fair-haired sons of bitches.

~~~

Samuel Bowles
Historian

All the people west of the Rocky Mountains feel a
peculiar personal pride in San Francisco, and, if
they would confess it, look forward to no greater
reward in death than to come hither.

~~~

Albert Bernard de Russailh
French Gold Rush forty-niner

There are honest women in San Francisco,
but not many.

Hubert Howe Bancroft
Early historian,
describing a gambling house of the 1850s

In one, the ceiling, rich in fresco and gilt, was
supported by glass pillars, pendant from which were
great chandeliers. Entering at night from the unlighted
dismal street into an immense room lighted with
dazzling brilliance and loud with the mingled sound of
musical instruments, the clink of coin and glasses, and
the hum of human voices, was like passing from the
dark depths to celestial brightness.

Robert Louis Stevenson
Author and early resident, circa 1880

The San Francisco Stock Exchange
was the place that continuously pumped
up the savings of the lower classes into
the pockets of the millionaires.

Sir George Simpson
Governor-general of Her Majesty's Hudson's Bay
Territories, on sailing into San Francisco Bay in 1841

Here on the very threshold of the country was
California in a nutshell.
Nature doing everything and
man doing nothing. . . .

Kevin Starr
Historian

San Francisco was zero in 1848, a Mexican village.
And in 1870 it was the tenth-largest city in the
United States. It was never your average American
city. San Francisco, right from the start, was a
second chance, a new beginning.

～～～～～

William A. Kelley
Early 1900s visitor

In San Francisco nothing is natural—
everything is forced; it is a hotbed where
all pursuits are stimulated by the fierce fire
of one predominant lust. . . .
the world's progress furnishes no parallel for the
precocious depravity of San Francisco.

～～～～～

Anonymous writer
In the Argonaut, 1870

When a San Franciscan gets to be immensely
wealthy, he builds a palace of a stable
with marble halls, Brussels carpets,
and hot and cold water in every stall;
a Chicago millionaire builds
a college.

J. B. Priestley
Novelist, and frequent visitor

These San Franciscans openly and heartily
enjoyed themselves. . . . They were like
advance specimens of a new tall pagan race.
They were also rather like large children.

~~~~~~

Hinton Helper
Late 19th century visitor

I have seen purer liquors,
better segars [*sic*], finer tobacco,
truer guns and pistols, larger dirks and
bowie knives, and prettier courtesans
here in San Francisco than in any
other place I have ever visited;
and it is my unbiased opinion that
California can and does furnish
the best bad things that are
obtainable in America.

~~~~~~

Anonymous writer
In the 1880s

In the space of one block on Kearny,
I could raise a gang to hijack a schooner,
topple a statue, rob a bank or set off for a
treasure hunt to the Galápagos.

Lucius Beebe
Writer, historian, and bon vivant

A contemporary advertisement
for a downtown shop listed
Colt's Patent revolvers at $30 to $40 apiece,
Sazerac brandy, fine French champagne,
and "white kid gloves of superior
quality at $1 for half the pair."
The San Francisco boulevardier who
packed a Colt wore white kid gloves
to avoid powder burns.

~~~~~~~~~

Mrs. Frank Leslie
Early social commentator

It has been said that in other cities
the *demimonde* imitates
the fashions of the *beau monde*,
but that in San Francisco the case
is reversed.

~~~~~~~~~

Headline
*From the San Francisco Examiner
circa 1880*

EATEN BY SHARKS
SAD ENDING TO A
DAY'S PLEASURE

Sally Stanford
San Francisco's
best-known madam

They were a wonderful
set of burglars, the people
who were running San Francisco
when I first came to town in
1923, wonderful because,
if they were stealing,
they were doing it with
class and style.

~~~~~~~

Mayor Roger Lapham
In 1947

The cable cars must go.
They're outmoded, expensive,
and inefficient.

~~~~~~~

Leland Stanford
Robber baron,
planning with his wife to
build Stanford University
in memorial to their son

The children of California
shall be our children.

Alan Watts
Philosopher, and Bay Area resident, on the 1960s

The Beat Generation was aggressively dowdy and slovenly, and lacked *gaieté d'esprit*. Patrons of the Coexistence Bagel Shop on Grant Avenue went about in shaggy bluejeans with their feet bare and grimy and their hair in a ponytail, and overuse of marijuana made them withdrawn and morose, even if externally beatific.

*Gertrude Stein named the Lost Generation
and Jack Kerouac named the Beat Generation.
On January 24, 1967,
police chief*
Thomas Cahill
confronted a group of hippies

You're sort of
the Love Generation,
aren't you?

———— ~ ————

Charles Perry
*Associate editor of Rolling Stone,
describing Haight Street during the 1967
"Summer of Love"*

Part Old Calcutta,
   with beads and paisley-print
      fabrics and bare feet, incense
      and tinkling anklet bells,
      beggars squatting
      on the sidewalk.
Part football stadium crush,
   complete with people
      selling programs . . .
Part Middle Ages,
   with a husband-and-wife
      evangelist team
      haranguing
      the crows.

CHAPTER 2

The Arts of Life

~~~~~~~

Bernard Maybeck
Architect, Palace of Fine Arts

If a Greek temple, pure and beautiful in lines
and color, were placed on the face of a placid lake,
surrounded by high trees and lit up by a glorious full
moon, you would recall the days when your mother
pressed you to her bosom . . . a protecting spirit
hovering over you warm and large. You have
there the point of transition from sadness
to content, which comes pretty near
to the total impression of the
Fine Arts Palace and lake.

Frank Lloyd Wright
Noted San Francisco architect

Early in my life, being very sure of my star, I had to choose between honest arrogance and hypocritical humility. I chose honest arrogance, and I'm still at it.

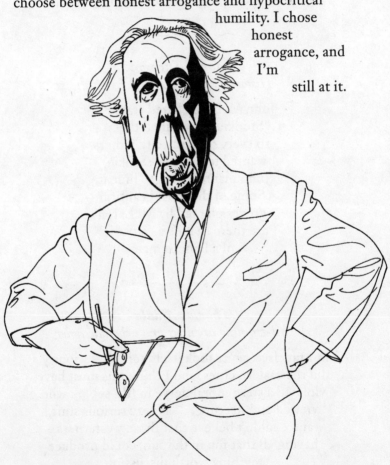

Advice to John McLaren
Designer of Golden Gate Park, from his father

Me boy, if ye have nothing to do,
go plant a tree and it'll grow while ye sleep.

Samuel Dickson
Historian, about John McLaren

John McLaren hated statues—
"Stookies!" he called them—
so every time the city fathers
wanted to plant a "stookie,"
John planted trees to hide it.
Some of the most beautiful
groves planted by McLaren
are there to hide a "stookie"
of a famous man.

Thomas Aidala
Award-winning architect and urban designer

San Francisco never took itself quite so seriously as
did the eastern cities, and I think this must have
violated a stern moral nerve in [those] . . . who
viewed architecture . . . as very serious stuff,
and couldn't believe that those westerners,
having all that fun in the sun, could produce
anything worth discussion.

Trader Vic
(Victor Bergeron)
Patron to
San Francisco sculptor Benny Bufano

He was a magnificent artist, a giant,
the finest sculptor of the age, and
the biggest pain in the neck
I ever met.

~~~~~~

The Very Reverend Alan Jones
Dean of San Francisco's Grace Cathedral

The arts are inherently dangerous and
destabilizing. A work of art invites you
to wonder and leaves you wondering.
Those who are eager to censor
the arts cannot stand their
ambiguity—
when we look at a
painting, see a play, or
listen to a piece of music,
we expect the work of art to
be immediately accessible.
It doesn't work that way.
Sometimes it takes great effort.
That is why art is "godly."
It is godly in that it will not give
in to easy and shallow
interpretation.

Isadora Duncan
Native San Franciscan and innovator of modern dance

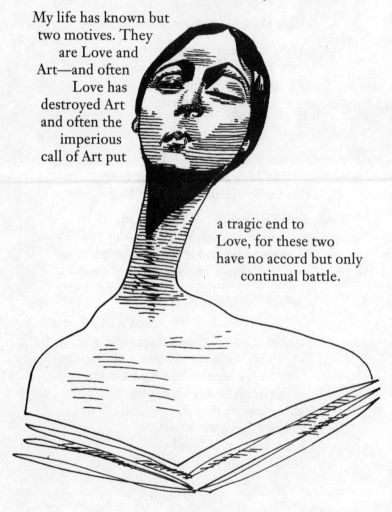

My life has known but
two motives. They
are Love and
Art—and often
Love has
destroyed Art
and often the
imperious
call of Art put

a tragic end to
Love, for these two
have no accord but only
continual battle.

CHAPTER 3
Bon Appétit

~~~~~~

Mary Austin
*Writer, early 1900s, recounting her visit to
Coppa's, the favored den of Bohemia*

One dined so well in San Francisco in those days.
Such heaping platefuls of fresh shrimps for appetizers!
Such abalone chowder, such savory and melting
sand dabs, salads so crisp, vegetables in such
profusion, and pies so deep and flaky.
Such dago red, fruity, sharp and warming!
And all for 35 cents!

Herb Caen
San Francisco Chronicle columnist

San Francisco can be a perfectly maddening city.
But when there's a good bar across the street,
almost any street, and a decent restaurant
around almost any corner, we are
not yet a lost civilization.

～～～～～

Herbert Gold
San Francisco writer

Perhaps the way the restaurants live
together on Balboa provides a clue to
what happens inevitably, in due course,
this being San Francisco and America.
The Chinese "No MSG" restaurants
press in among the Russian, Filipino,
Italian, and Just Plain Mom's places.
There is a certain energy of competition.
Eventually competition gives way to
living and let live, piroshki and dim sum.
And then you have a harmonious
equilibrium once more—
you find shrimp ravioli—
until the Martians arrive
in their spaceships
and start the whole process all over again.

M. F. K. Fisher
Food writer, and frequent San Francisco visitor

I still think that one of the pleasantest of all emotions is to know that I, I with my brain and hands, have nourished my beloved few, that I have concocted a stew or a story, a rarity or a plain dish, to sustain them truly against the hungers of the world.

Hank Greenwald
Broadcast commentator
for San Francisco Giants
baseball games

I always try to eat
a well-balanced meal
at Candlestick.
I put the cheeseburger
on one side, french
fires on the other, and
a coke in the middle.

~~~~~~

Howard Bulka
Chef at Earl's Restaurant

There's a certain naïveté
some people [in San Francisco]
have thinking that
food is always perfect,
service is hopping,
the crowd looks good,
the martini is perfectly chilled
and perfectly stirred,
and if you drop your fork,
there's another one in front
of you instantly.
When all that does come together,
it's not just a dinner.
That's a miracle.

Alice Waters
Bay Area chef
and owner of
Chez Panisse

I basically like things pretty informal. . . .
Sensual with lots of food. . . .
In order to do something simply,
you just have to have impeccable
ingredients that are picked out
of the garden that day. They
have that life about them that
speaks for itself.

CHAPTER 4

A Bridge of Gold

An August 18, 1869, edict from
Emperor Norton
A deranged but much beloved derelict
from the Gold Rush

We, Norton I, **Del Gratia,**
Emperor of the United States
and Protector of Mexico,
do order and direct . . .
that a suspension bridge
be constructed from
the improvements lately ordered
by our royal decree at
Oakland Point to Yerba Buena [Island]
from thence to the mountain range of Saucilleto [*sic*],
and from thence to the Farallones. . . .
Whereof fail not under pain of death!

Joseph B. Strauss
Chief engineer of the Golden Gate Bridge

The value of an idea depends not only on
the sweat you put into thinking it up, but also
on the sweat you put into getting people
to recognize and accept it.

―――――――

From a poem written by
Strauss
upon completion of the Golden Gate Bridge

At last the mighty task is done;
Resplendent in the western sun,
The bridge looms mountain high;
Its titan peers grip ocean floor,
Its great steel arms link shore with shore,
Its towers pierce the sky.

―――――――

Brett Bankie
*Park ranger, Golden Gate National Recreation Area,
after taking a group of inner-city students on a coastal
walk within sight of the Golden Gate Bridge*

They gasped in astonishment in virtual unison. It was
the view. They were almost hypnotized by it. Most of
these kids have never been this close to the bridge.
Nobody has ever told them they can come here
for free and walk across a bridge they've only
seen from far away or in pictures.

CHAPTER 5

From Victorians to High-Rises

~~~~~~~~~

Lewis Mumford
Writer and critic

The Transamerica "pyramid" exhibits the
essentially archaic and regressive nature of
the science fiction mind.

~~~~~~~~~

Sunset Magazine

Call them hats or hat racks,
San Francisco's newest high-rises sport
a variety of distinctively shaped tops—
pyramids to gables to steps—
that are visibly changing
the skyline.

Reyner Banham
Historian

San Francisco was plugged into California from the sea; the Gold Rush brought its first population and their culture around Cape Horn; their prefabricated Yankee houses and New England (or European) attitudes were dumped unmodified on the Coast.

~~~~~~

Barbara Bladen and Bill Porter
*Former owners of a landmark Victorian on
Steiner Street between Hayes and Grove*

It wasn't the twelve buses a day that revved their motors in front of the house while tourists took pictures. It wasn't seeing our house pictured on the phone-book cover, shopping bags, postcards, plastic place mats, and sales brochures. It wasn't photographers shooting models on our doorstep without permission. What finally drove us out was being asked for our autographs because Clint Eastwood lived there in *The Dead Pool* and love trysts in *Tales of the City* took place on the park bench directly in front of the house. Strangers were so curious about the interior that they would ring our doorbell and ask to be invited in as if it were a movie set.
We were a shooting gallery
for shutterbugs.

Elizabeth Pomada
*Author
and literary agent*

Thousands of homeowners
have transformed San Francisco
into the most colorful city
in the world. If there were
a Nobel prize for turning
dead architecture into works of art,
it would go to the homeowners,
colorists, interior designers,
and craftspeople
of San Francisco.

~~~~~

Ben Swig
*San Francisco civic leader,
in 1946*

You've got to
live modern.
You've got to
think big to be big.
The whole
San Francisco skyline
is going to change.
We're going to become
a second New York.

CHAPTER 6

Cultural and Sexual Diversity

~~~~~~~

JoAnne Davidson
Journalist

Where else but in San Francisco
    would characters such as Sister Boom-Boom,
        a transvestite who dresses in a
            miniskirted nun's habit,
            and a punk rocker named Jello Biafra
    run for seats on the Board of Supervisors?
And where else would 75,000 runners
        dress like centipedes, gorillas, and
            six packs of beer to participate in the
                "moving masquerade ball,"
            otherwise known as the
        Bay to Breakers Race?

Randy Shilts
San Francisco journalist and author

When heterosexuals
start hiding their wedding rings,
I'll hide the fact that I'm gay.

Harvey Milk
San Francisco supervisor

Turn that anger and frustration and madness
into something positive so that hundreds
will step forward, so that gay doctors
will come out, gay lawyers, gay judges,
gay bankers, gay architects.

Zohn Artman
A friend of Harvey Milk

You heard about Harvey's funeral?
They went out on a boat.
They wrapped his ashes in a
Doonesbury comic strip!
And then they put the ashes in a box,
and on the box in sequins it said "R.I.P."
They threw it overboard,
followed by some bubble bath.
There was a lot of humor,
'cause he was a really wonderful, funny guy.

Amy Tan
Novelist and
San Francisco resident

. . . we end up deliberately choosing the American things—hot dogs and apple pie— and ignoring the Chinese offerings. For a week, I even slept with a clothespin on my nose, hoping to alter my Asian appearance. . . . I've achieved a lifelong dream that once seemed to me as preposterous as a Chinese girl [from San Francisco] becoming president of the United States.

Samuel Dickson
Writer, describing the early 1900s

Chinatown at night! The most fascinating part of
Chinatown's night is the sight of hundreds of Chinese
children milling through the streets, home from night
school—Chinese children and Chinese babies
eating licorice strings and ice-cream
cornucopias and singing jive.

Armistead Maupin
San Francisco author

Once you're out of the closet you become the mother
or father confessor to the entire world. An open
homosexual is the perfect person to tell your
darkest secrets to, so your straight
friends tell you
the most
amazing
things.

Alice Walker
San Francisco's most acclaimed novelist

I feel safe with women. No woman
has ever beaten me up. No woman has
ever made me afraid
on the street.
I think that the
culture that
women put out
into the world
is safer for
everyone.

CHAPTER 7

All the City's a Stage

Homer Henley
*Writer for the Argonaut, recalling the 1932 opening
of the San Francisco Opera House*

Neither the play nor the players were the thing at the
gala opening of the new War Memorial Opera House;
it was the audience, the building itself, and most of all,
the spirit of San Francisco, the best-beloved city on the
continent. There was in that excited and brilliant
gathering a large proportion of direct descendants of
the Argonauts. . . . It was San Francisco's night, the
greatest artistic night she has ever known, and her
children paid her the homage of a love that has
survived every trial that such physical misfortunes
as fire, earthquakes, and famine can impose.
Our city has at last . . . the only municipally owned
opera house in America . . . probably the
finest opera house in the world.

Carol Doda
San Francisco's infamous topless dancer

The men acted like they had never
seen a pair of boobs before. . . . I knew if
I wanted people to keep coming to see me,
I'd have to give them a little something extra.
And I did. I got one [silicon] shot a week
in each breast for 20 weeks—sort
of like going to a gas station and
saying, "Fill'er up, Mack." . . .
People used to literally come in
[to the Condor nightclub]
week after week
just to see me grow.

~~~~~~~

Lenny Bruce
Nightclub comic

The first time I got arrested for obscenity
was in San Francisco.

~~~~~~~

Shirley Temple Black
*Former child film star and
San Francisco Bay Area resident*

I class myself with Rin Tin Tin. People in the
Depression wanted something to cheer them up,
and they fell in love with a dog and a little girl.

31

Barnaby Conrad
Writer, artist, and former nightclub owner,
in his book Name Dropping

The fifties were an incredible epoch in
San Francisco, a golden age for cabaret and
nightlife in the Barbary Coast and
North Beach areas. Fifty feet east from
the Matador on Broadway was
Ann's 440 Club, where
Johnny Mathis was discovered.
Across the street was the
Swiss-American hotel where
Lenny Bruce decided to fly out of
a second-story window with
nonfatal if predictable results.
A couple of blocks south at 599 Jackson Street,
Enrico Banducci's Hungry i welcomed
Mike Nichols and Elaine May, Woody Allen,
Bill Cosby, Jonathan Winters, Mort Sahl,
and a completely unknown singer named
Barbra Streisand. Of the latter,
I remember Banducci urging me,
"You gotta see this incredible dame—
nose like a trombone, voice like an angel!"
In one small section were great little
places like Tosca Café, the Bodega,
12 Adler Place, the Black Cat,
and the Purple Onion. . . .
The whole area was jumping,
it was safe, and it was gay in the
antiquated sense of the word.

Bill Graham
San Francisco rock concert promoter

We have to accept the reality that the musician is no longer a social force. He began to be one in the sixties and was one in the seventies. I'm not saying a positive or a negative force, but he was a force. Jimi Hendrix put a bandanna around his knee, and a million young guys did that. Jim Morrison took off his pants and wasn't wearing any underwear, and a lot of young people stopped wearing underwear.

~~~~~~~~~~

Jimi Hendrix
Rock musician

Once I was playing away [in San Francisco] and there was a short circuit and the guitar went up in flames. It went over pretty well, so for three times after that I sprayed lighter fluid on it and then stamped out the burning pieces.
When we played in the Hollywood Bowl, they were waiting for us with fire extinguishers.

~~~~~~~~~~

Phyllis Diller
Comedienne, who at 73 volunteered to be a poster girl for San Francisco's MUNI transit system

Think of me as a sex symbol for the men who gave up.

William Ball
*Founder of San Francisco's
American Conservatory Theater*

An actor is like a runner—
he has to sweat.

———~~~———

Jerry Herman
*Playwright, about actress and San Franciscan
Carol Channing*

Dolly was an overwhelming success.
But Carol said, "Jerry, we've got to
get one terrible review. . . .
You're only credible if
one person dislikes you."

———~~~———

Don Sherwood
*Highest-paid disc jockey on the West Coast
in the fifties and sixties*

I'm just a shaggy cool breeze in broadcasting.
I got that way hating people. I also hate
children, flowers, dogs, and housewives.
I've been trying to find myself for 32 years.
I haven't been fitting in. . . .
Whenever I got a new job
I got married to celebrate.

Pierre Moneux
*Director of the San Francisco Symphony
from 1935 to 1952, about symphonygoers
who complained he'd been there too long*

I don't blame them.
If I had to look at the same backside for 18 years,
I'd start complaining too.

~~~~~~~~

Herbert Blomstedt
*Director of the San Francisco Symphony
from 1985 to 1993, on how to gain
the respect of the orchestra*

One way used to be to be a tyrant.
Another way is to be a good buddy.
Neither way works well. I think sheer
professionalism—to be very well prepared
and a very good musician—is the best way.
And it helps to have a working
understanding of psychology.

~~~~~~~~

Luisa Tetrazzini
*San Francisco's all-time favorite soprano,
breaking her New York contract*

I will sing in San Francisco if I have to sing in the
streets, for I KNOW THE STREETS OF SAN
FRANCISCO ARE FREE.

Robin Williams
Film actor and San Francisco resident

You have to pull back and recharge. You have to meet
people outside the movies—there's a whole other
world. Not everybody is worrying about grosses and
points. That's why it's great to be outside Hollywood,
where you're confronted by your career every five
minutes. Instead, you're confronted by other things—
like no heating. The furnace breaks, and
I become Father Man.

Kurt Herbert Adler
General director of the
San Francisco Opera, 1953 to 1981

Opera is always a gamble.
There is a big cemetery of operas.
But on the way to the cemetery
the cortege can at least be seen—
and, who knows, even stopped.

<hr>

Lofti Mansouri
General director of the
San Francisco Opera

There are still temperamental singers,
and thank God! That's what makes
opera exciting. Without temperament,
it would be nothing.

<hr>

Tony Walton
Designer for the
San Francisco Ballet

There is still a sexy fluidity in the dancing.
The dancers have a range of genuine styles—
not stylization—so broad it's almost random.
People work with so much relish it borders on
disrespect in the eyes of pious observers.

Johnny Mathis
Singer and native San Franciscan

To sing my songs I have to say the innermost thoughts
of my heart—each line, each phrase, I have to live or
die by. I get annoyed at myself for sounding forlorn . . .
so lonely . . . that I'm
almost pitiful.
I actually feel
that way.

Tony Kornheiser
Writer, about San Francisco singer
Johnny Mathis in 1990

He's 54 but it's as if he stopped aging in 1965,
as if his end of the bargain was to always sound the
same, and God's end of the bargain was to guarantee
Mathis would look the same for eternity. In the
audience, a man about the same age turns to his
companion and asks, "How come he looks so
young, and I look like my dentist?"

~~~~~~~~~~

Francis Ford Coppola
San Francisco filmmaker

I was always impressed that when
Genghis Khan died, his last question was,
"Was I a good man or a bad man?"
I want to be a good man.
I want to be a hero.

~~~~~~~~~~

Lofti Mansouri
General director of the San Francisco Opera

Opera is the greatest art form. . . .
It is like a fabulous dish, if one little
spice is wrong, the ensemble—
the whole thing—won't be quite right.
When everything goes right, it's like a miracle.

Raymond Burr
Actor and Bay Area resident

The TV series "Perry Mason" educated many people in the country who knew nothing of the law. . . .
But once it started Perry took over. It became a burden. . . . Mason never once, in nine years, had a sense of humor. . . . Mason never once, in nine years, had a single good friend. Mason never once had a home to go to.

Michael Smuin
Former director of the
San Francisco Ballet Company

Don't you think people are a little tired of
Swan Lake?

~~~~~~

Marilyn Monroe
To former baseball outfielder and native San
Franciscan Joe DiMaggio after returning from
entertaining the troops in Korea

Joe, you've never heard such cheering.
His reply: Yes I have.

~~~~~~

Barbara Bladen
Drama critic for San Francisco newspapers

Better to be a critic in San Francisco for the
wanna-bes than in New York for the has-beens.
There's a vitality in the performing and visual arts
here that matches the creative verve of Paris in
the twenties and thirties. There's a minimum of
mainstream entertainment, maybe because there
are no tired old businessmen to be amused.
San Francisco is a young person's town;
you have to be able to keep up with
the fast-changing new trends and
dynamic spirit of adventure.

Tony Bennett
Singer, discussing one of the world's most popular songs

Ralph Sharon and I thought that "I Left My Heart In San Francisco" would just be a local hit in the Bay Area. But we had a tip-off that it might be bigger than that. We were in Hot Springs, Arkansas, on our way to San Francisco. We were rehearsing the song and the bartender there said to me, "Hey, kid, if you record this song, I'll buy the record."

Steve Silver
*Originator of North Beach's
long-running
Beach Blanket Babylon*

Surf's up!
Beach Blanket Babylon
is like a spa—
you forget your problems,
forget your troubles,
and you laugh . . .

~~~~~~~~

George Cory
*Songwriter for
"I Left My Heart in San Francisco"*

We might have left our heart there,
but the money
[$50,000 a year in royalties]
is here.

CHAPTER 8

Ruminations of the Literati

~~~~~~

Frank Norris
Novelist, in 1897

Kearny Street, Montgomery Street, Nob Hill,
Telegraph Hill, of course Chinatown, Lone
Mountain, the Poodle Dog, the Palace Hotel
and the What Cheer House, the Barbary Coast,
the Crow's Nest, the Mission, the Bay, the
Bohemian Club, the Presidio, Spanish Town,
Fisherman's Wharf. There is an indefinable air
about all these places that is suggestive of stories at
once. You fancy the names would look well on
a book's page. The people who frequent them
could walk right into a novel or short story
and be at home.

Ambrose Bierce
Early columnist in the San Francisco Examiner, circa 1870

Good-bye. If you hear of my being stood against a Mexican stone wall and shot to rags, please know that I think it a pretty good way to depart this life. It beats old age, disease, or falling down the cellar stairs. To be a Gringo in Mexico—ah, that is euthanasia!

Joaquin Miller's
first words upon
getting off the boat
in San Francisco
in 1870

Let us go and
talk with the poets

~~~~~~~~

Ambrose Bierce
Early columnist in
the San Francisco Examiner

The Hearst [publishing] method
has all the reality of masturbation.

~~~~~~~~

Gertrude Atherton,
San Francisco novelist,
writing about Ambrose Bierce

His column, "Prattle,"
in the *San Francisco Examiner*
was brilliant, scarifying, witty, bitter,
humorous, and utterly fearless. He was
no respecter of persons, and many of the
"eminents" when honored by his notice in
that column must have felt as if they were
taking a long draft of gall and wormwood.
We were always expecting to hear that shot.

Robert Frost
Poet and native San Franciscan,
recalling picnicking at Bakers Beach as a boy

The shattered water made a misty din.
Great waves looked over others coming in
And thought of doing something to the shore
That water never did to land before.
The clouds were low and hairy in the skies. . . .
It looked as if a night of dark intent
was coming, and not only a night, an age. . . .

~~~~~~~~~~

Jack Kerouac
San Francisco writer, in On the Road,
describing the 1960s "flower children"

They danced down the streets like dingle-dodies,
and I shambled after as I've been doing all
my life after people who interest me,
because the only people for me
are the mad ones,
the ones who are mad to live,
mad to talk, mad to be saved, desirous
of everything at the same time, the ones who
never yawn or say a commonplace thing,
but burn, burn, burn like fabulous yellow
Roman candles exploding like spiders
across the stars and in the middle
you see the blue centerlight pop
and everybody goes
"Awww!"

William Saroyan
Author, and part-time San Francisco resident

San Francisco itself is
art, above all literary
art. . . . Every block is
a short story, every
hill a novel.
Every
home is
a poem,
every
dweller
within
immortal.
That is the
whole truth.

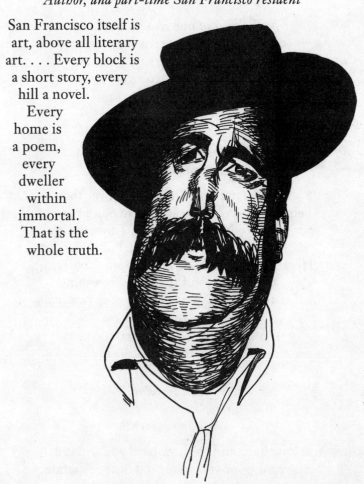

George Sterling
Poet laureate of San Francisco

At the end of our streets is sunrise;
At the end of our streets are spars;
At the end of our streets is sunset;
At the end of our streets are stars.

~~~~~~

Gertrude Atherton
San Francisco novelist

It took me little time to discover that
belonging to the best society in San Francisco
cut no ice in New York. One of my candid sins
was that I had not made my debut in *Century*,
Harper's, *Scribner's*, or *The Atlantic Monthly* . . .
but in the San Francisco *Argonaut*.
I realized even then that the only revenge
worth having is success.

~~~~~~

Jack London
*Novelist and native San Franciscan,
recalling his youth*

You look back and see how hard you worked,
and how poor you were, and how desperately
anxious you were to succeed, and all you can
remember is how happy you were.

Allen Ginsberg
Poet, in the opening lines of "Howl"

I saw the best minds of my generation destroyed
by madness; starving, hysterical, naked, draggin
themselves through the negro streets at dawn
looking for an angry fix. . . .

———

John Steinbeck
*California-born writer and
frequent San Francisco resident*

Once I knew the City very well, spent my attic days
there, while others were being a lost generation in
Paris, I fledged in San Francisco, climbed its hills,
slept in its parks, worked on its docks, marched
and shouted in its revolts. . . . It had been kind
to me in the days of my poverty and it did
not resent my temporary solvency.

———

Danielle Steel
*Top-of-the-charts novelist,
after buying a landmark mansion
built by Adolph Spreckels*

There is absolutely no glamour at all
to my sitting over the typewriter for
twenty hours, drinking cold Sanka
and eating Oreo cookies.

Virginia Blair
Speaking to the
Tenderloin Women's
Writers Group

Writing is nothing to be ashamed of
as long as you do it in private and
wash your hands afterwards.

~~~~~~~~~~

William Randolph Hearst
Publisher,
San Francisco Examiner

Ethics are the consolation
of weak men.

~~~~~~~~~~

George P. West
A contemporary of
William Randolph Hearst

The *Examiner* office was a madhouse inhabited
by talented and erratic young men, drunk
with life in a city that never existed before
or since. They had a mad boss, one who
flung away money, like a ruler of the late
Empire at his house above the water at
Sausalito, and cheered them on as
they made newspaper history.

Belva Davis
KRON television reporter

Infotainment is
crowding journalism out.
News, in the sense that
we understood it a decade ago,
isn't on the drawing board;
it's not even in the
development stage.

~~~~~~

Jerry George
*Development director
and publisher of
Whole Earth Books
in the Bay Area*

It's interesting to watch people
who spend all their time
communicating electronically.
They lose the ability to
read body language and
voice intonations.
Yelling consists of using
all capital letters.

CHAPTER 9

Quake, Rattle, and Roll

~~~~~~~

Fray Juan Crespi
Missionary, describing a severe 1800s earthquake

It lasted half as long as an Ave Maria.

~~~~~~~

Mark Twain
Writing about the quake of 1865

Such another destruction of mantel ornaments and
toilet bottles as the earthquake created, San Francisco
never saw before. Hardly an individual escaped nausea
entirely. A lady sitting in her rocking and quaking
parlor saw the wall part at the ceiling, open and
shut twice like a mouth, and then drop the end
off a brick on the floor like a tooth. She was
a woman easily disgusted with foolishness,
and she arose and went out of there.

Will Irwin
Journalist, 1906

It is as though a pretty,
frivolous woman had passed
through a great tragedy.
She survives, but she is
sobered and different.
If it rises out of the ashes
it must be a modern city,
much like other cities and
without its old atmosphere.

~~~~~~~

The Oregonian
12 April 1906

Caste and social standing were nothing. . . .
Six days after the disaster, I saw a man dressed
in evening coat and waistcoat, opera hat, blue
overalls, and a pair of logger's boots. He had
been one of an opera party Tuesday evening,
and in the panic all he could find was the upper
garments of his evening suit. The overalls and
boots he picked up later in his wanderings.
The appearance of this man was ludicrous
to a degree, yet he did not mind it. I saw him,
with his opera hat tilted far back on his head,
the bosom of his evening shirt smeared and stained,
cooking on the street for half a dozen refugees.
He was a man of means.

Mayor Gene Schmitz

Our fair city lies in ruins,
but those are the damndest,
finest ruins ever seen on
the face of the earth.

~~~~~~~~~

Enrico Caruso
Opera singer,
jolted from his bed at the Palace Hotel,
never came back

I'll take Vesuvius!

~~~~~~~~~

Herb Caen
San Francisco Chronicle columnist

From reading the record,
we know that all San Francisco
is divided into two parts:
the city that flowered before
the [1906] earthquake,
and the entirely different one
that rose from the flames.
What is not quite clear,
to this day, is what it was
that died in those flames,
but we suspect it was
something special.

Jerry Carroll
San Francisco Chronicle
columnist

There is no greater betrayal
than when the earth defaults
on the understanding
that it stay underfoot
while we go about the
business of life,
which is full of perils
as it is.

Charlotte Mailliard Swig
San Francisco's official hostess

Mayor Alioto had a tremendous
Earthquake Party in April 1969
for over 10,000. Earthquake hysteria
was building and we had a tongue-in-cheek
party for 200 at the Top of the Mark.
Lou Lurie, who owned the Mark Hopkins,
invited those people who could best restart
San Francisco in case of massive disaster.
There was one shoemaker, one laundry person,
47 bartenders, and only one politician.

～～～～～

Dick Draper
San Francisco Examiner sportswriter, 1989

Let it be noted that a stadium,
not the fans, did the wave.

～～～～～

Buck Hall
Motorist on the
Oakland/San Francisco Bay Bridge

The tunnel was moving,
all the cars were sliding around
like they were on ice.
The suspension cables were swinging
back and forth, like a giant harp
somebody was playing.

CHAPTER 10

Nearer My God to Thee

The Reverend Cecil Williams
Pastor of San Francisco's
Glide Memorial Church

People aren't looking for God.
God's looking for them.

Werner Erhard
Who founded est in
San Francisco in 1971

The secret was that *it* [life] is already together,
and what you have to experience is
experiencing it being together.

Alice Walker
San Francisco's most acclaimed novelist

It's so clear that you have to cherish everyone.
I think that's what I get from these
older black women, that sense that
every soul is to be cherished,
that every flower is to bloom.

~~~~~~

Alan Watts
Philosopher and Bay Area resident

My own feeling has always been that
in order to be a real person you must
know how to be a genuine fake.

~~~~~~

The Council
For the 1967 "Summer of Love"

This summer the youth of the world are making
a holy pilgrimage to our city, to affirm and
celebrate a new spiritual dawn. . . .
The activity of the youth of the nation
which has given birth to the Haight-Ashbury
is a small part of a worldwide spiritual awakening.
Our city has become the momentary focus of this
awakening. It is a gift from God which we
may take, nourish, and treasure.

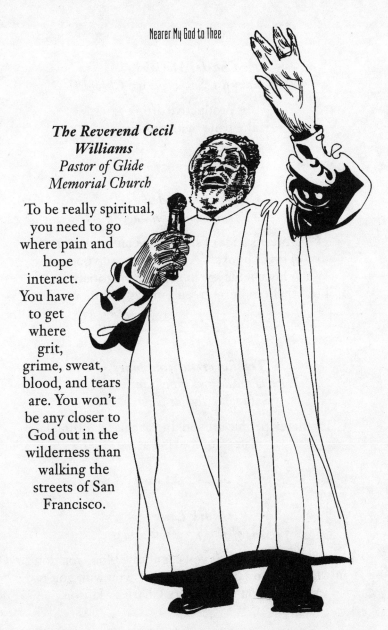

The Reverend Cecil Williams
Pastor of Glide Memorial Church

To be really spiritual, you need to go where pain and hope interact. You have to get where grit, grime, sweat, blood, and tears are. You won't be any closer to God out in the wilderness than walking the streets of San Francisco.

Charles McCabe
1970s columnist, San Francisco Chronicle

A productive drunk
is the bane of all moralists.

~~~~~~~~

Bonnie Nadell
San Francisco literary agent

God means a lot of six-figure contracts and
lots of great books. . . . I tend toward voodoo.
When my clients are in contract negotiations,
I tell them to burn green candles [for money].

~~~~~~~~

The Reverend Jim Jones
Prior to the demise of his San Francisco
People's Temple Church

Too many people are looking at this [the Bible]
instead of looking at *me*.

~~~~~~~~

Mark Lane
One of Jim Jones's attorneys

Jones became a devil. If you cannot be God, you don't
just fall back to rank and file. . . . If you win, you're
Moses, if you lose, you're Charles Manson.

Art Hoppe
San Francisco Chronicle columnist

Most people believe the afterlife is
one of eternal bliss. The only
thing I've never understood
is why my devout San
Francisco friends
are invariably so
reluctant to get there.

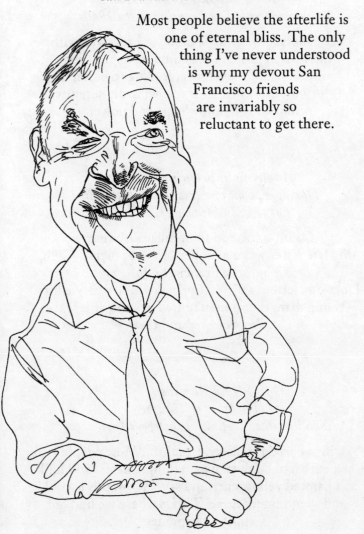

Grace Slick
Singer and Bay Area resident,
remembering San Francisco in the 1960s

The message that we sought, and received with
intensity, was that life should be a sprawling,
unpredictable adventure, leading to either a
glorious, early death, or to a wizardly serenity
coupled with knowledge and power.

~~~~~~

Anonymous prominent matron
During a phone conversation with an editor
at the San Francisco Chronicle

I want a correction of today's obituary.
My late sister was a member of the Francisc*a* Club,
not the Francisc*o* Club.
Does one letter really matter? asked the weary editor.
Young man, the woman huffed, it's the difference
between *cod* and *God*.

~~~~~~

Ed Riggins
Publisher of Thrasher,
San Francisco's definitive skateboard magazine

Skating is urban transcendentalism. Most people look
at a curb and don't think anything. Skaters will look
at a painted yellow curb and say, "Wow, this is cool,"
and spend hours there. This is where we find our
spiritual happiness.

CHAPTER II

Clothes Make the Man

~~~~~~~~

Oscar Wilde
*British author and frequent San Francisco visitor,
in 1882, about the San Francisco Bohemian Club*

I never saw so many well-dressed, well-fed,
business-looking Bohemians in my life.

~~~~~~~~

Wilkes Bashford
*Clothier, about California House Speaker
and San Francisco native Willie Brown*

He's the closest thing
to an emperor we have.
He's regal and he's in control of
everything he sees.

George Zimmer
*CEO of Men's Wearhouse
clothing chain in the
San Francisco Bay Area*

I'm proud to say we cover
the asses of the masses.

~~~~~~

Nicholas Graham
*San Francisco clothier
and owner of Joe Boxer*

I don't really know why I'm here.
I came ten years ago for a
weekend and I just stayed.
So I decided to start a business.
Buyers love coming here.
New York is so garmento.
And LA has its own acid-washed
version of garmento.
San Francisco is
not garmento.

CHAPTER 12

Socially Seen

~~~~~~~~

Pat Montandon
*San Francisco media personality and jet-setter
of the sixties and seventies*

Every girl in the world should know how to dance
beautifully, how to flirt successfully,
how to make love divinely—
and how to make crepes.

~~~~~~~~

Gardner Mein
*Third-generation San Franciscan,
on how to get into San Francisco society*

There are two ways. One is to marry well,
even if you have to get rid of your current wife
(or husband) to do so. The other way is to start a
charity, which will help you to glorify yourself
and get recognition.

S. McKeen
Socialite,
also on how to get into
San Francisco society

It's expensive.
If you're a bachelor,
have lots of "big boy toys."
Invest in a good tux—
never rent one—and wear it
with patent leather shoes.
Come with letters of reference
to top people in town.
You have to be attractive.
People will give parties
to introduce you.
Then you have
to entertain a lot.
And never, never
miss a disease ball.

~~~~~~~~

Rand Castle
Asian Art Museum director

When I have to deal with
bores [at parties] I look around
the room to see who else is
boring and I introduce them
to each other immediately.
They cancel each other out.

CHAPTER 13

Sports and Mayhem

~~~~~~

Dusty Baker
Manager of the San Francisco Giants

Black pride was important to my folks, but stressed more by my mom. She would tell us if you're a black American you have to be twice as good to attain the same thing. This is the philosophy I maintain at all times. I also realize when I'm managing out there, I'm not only managing for San Francisco. I'm managing for a lot of the people that are pulling for me.

~~~~~~

Joe DiMaggio
Former baseball outfielder and native San Franciscan, when asked why he gave his all in every game

Because there might be somebody out there who's never seen me play before.

Barry Bonds
San Francisco
Giants outfielder

In baseball, you get to see us,
 touch us, trade our cards,
buy and sell jerseys. To me,
 that dilutes the excitement. . . .
I'm supposed to stand out
 there for three hours and
then sign autographs?
 If fans pay $10 to see Batman,
they don't expect to get
 Jack Nicholson's autograph.

~~~~~~

Will Clark
Former San Francisco
Giants first baseman,
on how to autograph a baseball

Sign horizontally in what's
 called the "sweet spot."
 It's the widest point
 between the stitches.
 It makes a difference
 what type of pen you use.
 If you sign a leather ball,
 unless you use
 a ballpoint pen,
 it'll smudge.

Willie Mays
*Former San
Francisco Giants
outfielder*

I just finished
high school
and I had to go
into baseball to
support my family.
I couldn't say, "I'm
Willie Mays. Do
something for
me." I played 22
years in baseball,
andeverything
was done for me.

All I had to do was throw, catch, and hit.
I came out of baseball and went into
the business world, and I knew nothing.

71

Bill Walsh
Former football coach
of San Francisco 49ers

There were those
in our organization who
didn't think Joe Montana
would be an NFL starter. . . .
But when he was in sync,
he had an intuitive, instinctive
nature rarely equaled by
any athlete in any sport.

Joe Montana
Former quarterback
for the San Francisco 49ers,
about the miracle drive
that won Super Bowl XXIII

Did I say anything
   inspirational?
      Oh, no, I was concerned
      with other things.
         We were calling
         two plays at a time,
            and I had to think about
               what the second one would be.
            I did say to myself, though,
            "Here we go,
         just like Dallas in '82."

Jerry Rice
Wide receiver
for the San Francisco 49ers

I want to look good on the football field also.
The way I tape my shoes. The way I tuck my
shirt into my pants. My helmet has to be clean.
I also tuck this towel into my belt. I sit down
right before the start of the game and I write
my nickname, Flash 80, on it. The towel has
to be white. My shoes have to be white. My
socks have to come up to a certain length. . . .
Most . . . receivers try to be unique. . . .
And for me everything has to be neat.

~~~~~~

Roger Craig
Former running back
of the San Francisco 49ers

We're warriors.
The superstars on our team
set our standards high.
We stay in shape,
and we can overcome
nagging injuries. . . .
The team watches us
playing hurt or trying to
play hurt, and that rubs off
on the other players.

Scott Ostler
San Francisco Chronicle
sportswriter,
referring to the defeat
by Dallas in the
1993 NFC play-off game

The 49ers were
so badly flattened
that they didn't fly
back to San Francisco,
they were faxed.

~~~~~~~

Michael Murphy
Author and founder
of the world-famous Esalen Institute
in San Francisco and Monterey

You don't have to
bear down on your tennis
game like a stupid
Golden Gate Park duffer.
You just have to dream
yourself into the flow
of body, racket, ball,
net, and sweet
San Francisco air.

CHAPTER 14

Those Infamous Streets

A Gold Rush era sign
At the corner of Clay and Kearny

THIS STREET IS IMPASSABLE
NOT EVEN JACKASSABLE

Isadora Duncan
Native San Franciscan
and innovator of modern dance

When I was five we had a cottage on 23rd Street.
Failing to pay the rent, we could not remain
there but moved to 17th Street, and in a short
time, as funds were low, the landlord objected,
so we moved to 22nd Street, where we
were not allowed to live peacefully
but went to 10th Street. . . .

Helen Hunt Jackson
New England novelist, on visiting San Francisco in 1872

The street was as steep as the street of an Alpine village. Men and women walked up its sidewalks bowed over, as if nobody were less than ninety. Those walking down had their bodies slanted back and their knees projecting in front as people come down mountains. The horses went at a fast walk, almost a trot. On corners the driver reined them up, turned them at a sharp angle, and stopped them to breathe a minute. The hills rise so sharply and the houses are set on them at such incredible angles that it wouldn't surprise you, any day when you are watching it, to see the whole city slide down whole streets at a time.

~~~~~~~~

John Dos Passos
Novelist, in 1946

Whoever laid the town out took the conventional checkerboard pattern of streets and without the slightest regard for the laws of gravity planked it down on an irregular peninsula that was a confusion of steep slopes and sandhills. The result is exhilarating. Whenever you step out on the street there's a hilltop in one direction or the other. From the top of each hill you get a view and the sight of more hills to the right and left and ahead that offer the prospect of still broader views. The process goes on indefinitely. You can't help making your way painfully to the top of each hill to see what you can see.

Rob Morse
*San Francisco Chronicle
columnist*

Kearny Street—just avoid it and
take Sansome. Some old-timers say
"Kurny." A smaller
but perhaps
even older
group says
"Karny."
Younger
folks say
"Keerne."
I say the
hell with it.

Margot Patterson Doss
*Former San Francisco
Chronicle columnist and
San Francisco's best-known walker*

Our's is a more pleasurable place to
walk than most metropolitan places.
However, it gets less so every day.

~~~~~~~~~~

Allan Jacobs
*Author and city planner,
in 1994*

Three decades ago,
passage of a $25 million
beautification bond issue was
hailed as a way to transform
Market Street into a Champs-Elysées
of the West, a boulevard fancied with
granite gutters, designer ash cans, and
widened, brick-inlaid sidewalks.
Today, San Francisco's main drag
has been downgraded as a
might-have-been that has
lost its chance to be listed
as one of the world's
Great Streets.

CHAPTER 15

Winds of War

~~~~~~~~~

Jerry Carroll
San Francisco Chronicle columnist

The city worked when the boys came
marching home [in 1945] from making the
world safe for democracy again. Nobody spray
painted the walls, there weren't homeless
sitting in the doorways or shambling crazy
people everywhere you looked. Crack was
the sound a bat made hitting a baseball.
Taxes were low and optimism high.
People dressed up to go downtown.

~~~~~~~~~

Wartime motto
At San Francisco's Izzy Gomez's bar

Awake my little ones, and fill the cup,
before life's liquor in the cup be dry.

Frances Moffat
*Former San Francisco
Chronicle society editor*

For four years,
San Francisco was the front.
Temporary wooden barracks stood
across from the Opera House. . . .
Hundreds of soldiers were quartered
in temporary plywood cubicles in the
Fairmont, St. Frances, Palace, and
Mark Hopkins hotels. The city was the
embarkation point for thousands
of soldiers and marines who sailed
across the South Pacific to
invade Guadalcanal, Tarawa,
and Iwo Jima.

Tom Cole
Author, in his book, A Short History of San Francisco

Since the war, San Francisco
has been at the vanguard of
just about every new idea,
fad, political movement,
crackpot scheme,and
earnest effort to cope with
the befuddlements
of modern times . . .

CHAPTER 16

Political Jungle

Pat Conroy
Novelist, screenwriter, and San Francisco transplant

San Francisco has the meanest politics I've ever seen.
To be mayor here is a hard job. This is a combat
sport out here. Atlanta seems much more genteel.
This is hardball. I pray I don't do anything to piss
off ACT UP while I'm out here. When people
get upset at the politicians here I say, "Are you
shitting me?" Every one of them is
wonderful, open, and liberal. Of course,
I was raised in the South.

Dashiell Hammett
San Francisco novelist, early 1900s

Most things in San Francisco can be bought or taken.

Former Mayor Roger Dearborn Lapham
In 1946

The average San Franciscan's idea of government
is the average schoolboy's idea of school:
the less of it the better.

~~~~~~~

Former Mayor Joseph Alioto
In 1968 (who whether humming operatic airs,
sipping Campari and soda, or playing the violin,
wowed crowds in the ghetto)

The ghetto never goes to the Opera House,
so we'll take the inaugural to the ghetto.

~~~~~~~

Former Mayor Joseph Alioto

The big city mayor has the toughest job
in the country next to the presidency.
He walks on the edge of a volcano
that may erupt any moment.

~~~~~~~

Former Mayor George Moscone

As a practical matter, anybody who wants to knock
me off can do it regardless of whether I have
Dick Tracy or anybody else with me.

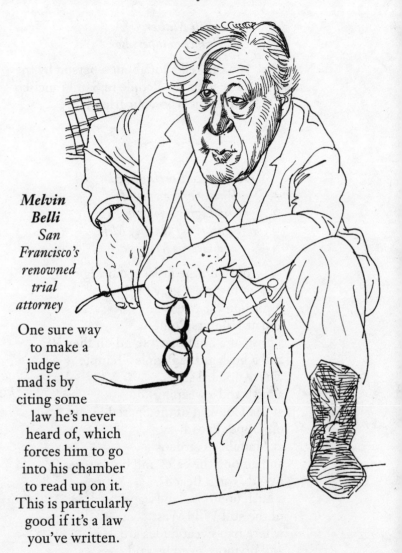

Melvin Belli *San Francisco's renowned trial attorney*

One sure way to make a judge mad is by citing some law he's never heard of, which forces him to go into his chamber to read up on it. This is particularly good if it's a law you've written.

Bill Maher
San Francisco supervisor

In New York you can tell a lot about a person by the
quality of his enemies. People in San Francisco
want to know who your friends are.

~~~~~~~~~~

Lawrence Ferlinghetti
*Writer and owner of
City Lights Bookstore,
on the deaths of Harvey Milk
and George Moscone*

. . . a hush on the great red bridge
and on the great gray bridge
A hush in the Mission
and at Hunters Point
a hush at a hot potato stand on Pier 39
and a hush at the Peoples Temple
where no bird sings
a hush and a weeping
at the Convent of the Sacred Heart
on Upper Broadway
at Mabuhay Gardens
and among the cafes and bookstores
of old North Beach
a hush upon the landscape
of the still Wild West
where two sweet dudes are dead
and no more need be said. . . .

Shirley Temple Black
*Former child film
star and San
Francisco Bay Area
resident, in her bid
for Congress*

Little Shirley Temple
is not running. . . .
I'm neither a
hawk nor a dove;
I'm an owl.

Willie Brown
*California House Speaker
and native San Franciscan on how to make a speech*

Select one or two people in the room—
regardless of how many are there—
and seduce them.

~~~~~~~

Mayor Frank Jordan

It is an outrage that the city would in any
way attempt to regulate poetry by permit.
Those of us who lived through the
Beat Generation say the Beat must go on.

"We don't care one whit
For poetry by permit
Let the verse flow free
From the beach to the sea
And uphold the tradition of Ferlinghetti."

~~~~~~~

Angela Alioto
*President of the San Francisco
Board of Supervisors*

My health is definitely
affected by politics.
I have to stop in at four
or five dinners a night!

Senator Dianne Feinstein
Former mayor of San Francisco in 1980

This city typifies the American dream of a sense of tolerance and openness with different people living closely together, carefully, with respect for the law, not impinging their will on others but living with a growing mutual respect.

Jerry Brown
Former governor of California, speaking to UC Berkeley political students in the spring of 1994, after his unsuccessful bid for the presidency

You will become cogs in a machine of deception and manipulation. . . . The people who are supposedly leading are cut off and living inside their own bell jar of privilege. . . . Because I've been an insider, I've done the sound bites, I know the lies, I know what a hype it all is.

CHAPTER 17

View Extravaganza

~~~~~~

Carole Woods
Nob Hill resident

Foghorns put me to sleep at night and the cable-car
bells wake me in the morning. From my living room
I can see Alcatraz and the Golden Gate Bridge.
Some days, I just sit at the window and stare.

~~~~~~

Brett Bankie
Park ranger, Golden Gate National Recreation Area

We have visitors whose best vistas at home are endless
fields of corn, all privately owned. Here they're seeing
the Pacific Ocean for the first time. They're looking at
water and sky. And they're thinking about ships,
seagulls, and whales, getting a sense of freedom
they've never known.

Angela Alioto
President of the San Francisco Board of Supervisors

San Francisco is more Italian than any other city I've been to in America. There's a little Vento. Coit Tower is very much like Monte Mario in Rome— the atmosphere, the view— or San Gimignano near Siena or other parts of Rome. Even easing into Chinatown, it has that very rococo Venetian effect and you feel it's like Venice. And Grant Avenue— it's right out of the Trastevere in Rome.

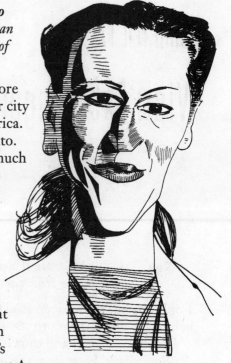

Fiorello LaGuardia
Mayor of New York 1935–1945, upon visiting San Francisco in 1943

God took the beauty of the Bay of Naples, the Vally of the Nile, the Swiss Alps, the Hudson River Valley, rolled them into one and made San Francisco Bay.

CHAPTER 18

Speaking Out on Anything and Everything

André Malrau
French minister of culture,
on hearing a San Franciscan refer to his city as
"The Paris of the West"

Ah, the touching arrogance of cities
born only yesterday.

Oscar Wilde
British author and
frequent San Francisco visitor

It's an odd thing, but anyone who disappears
is said to be seen in San Francisco.

Gertrude Atherton
San Francisco novelist,
when asked why she never remarried

I expected perfection and never found it.
And, of course, I wanted to be "understood."
All women want to be understood until they
understand themselves.

―――――

Ambrose Bierce
Early San Francisco
Examiner columnist

San Francisco . . .
that moral penal colony
of the world.

―――――

Helen Hunt Jackson
New England novelist,
on visiting California in 1872

San Francisco will never look like anything
but a toppling town. . . . Does anybody believe
that if the Pilgrims had landed in California,
witches would have been burned there?
Or that if gold strewed the ground today
from Cape Cod to Berkshire,
a Massachusetts man would spend
it like a San Franciscan?

Minerva
*Astrology columnist
for the San
Francisco
Chronicle*

San Francisco
is a Sagittarian,
free spirited
and volatile,
needing—
demanding!—
freedom to live on
the edge. Her Moon
is in Scorpio—ready
always to rise
magnificently
from her
own ashes.
Finally,
there's
Aquarius
rising,
assuring us
that what
San Francisco
thinks today
is tomorrow's
road map for
everyone else.

Rudyard Kipling
Author, circa 1850

San Francisco is a mad city inhabited
for the most part by perfectly insane people whose
women are of a remarkable beauty.

Will Durst
*King of the 1983 San Francisco Comedy Competition
and mayoral candidate*

In San Francisco,
Halloween is redundant.

Pastor P. T. Mammen
*President of the
San Francisco Association of Evangelicals*

San Francisco sets the trend
for defaming anything that is traditional.

Sally Stanford
*San Francisco's best-known madam,
in 1966 when she was rich and retired,
advising a young woman*

Get the money first, honey.
Get the money first.

Guy Wright
*San Francisco
Examiner
columnist*

San Francisco is a
fermentation vat for
oddball notions . . .
a city where
tolerance
deteriorates
into license.
A town without
a norm.

Joan Hitchcock
1960s socialite,
after slipping her breasts
from her gown and displaying
them to a photographer

They got me three husbands.
They'll get me more.

~~~~~~~

Ira A. Brown
San Francisco Superior Court judge

A woman told me in a complaint
that she wanted $30 trillion in
compensatory damages and
$30 trillion in general damages.
When I asked her how she arrived
at that figure, she said, "I was born
in the Year of the Tiger, and the
tiger is a cat, and a cat has nine lives.
And I want to get the damages
for all nine lives."

Herb Caen
*San Francisco Chronicle
columnist*

San Francisco learned how to
drink in the Gold Rush days
and has never stopped trying
to improve on the art.
Even the Bay has an
olive in it. . . .

~~~~~~~

John Aiken
*Director of the
San Francisco Zoo, discussing
Sishkiyou, a bald eagle*

She's a bit neurotic.
But then, she's had
a tragic childhood.

~~~~~~~

Carol Channing
Actress and native San Franciscan

With a female comic . . .
what she does isn't funny unless
it comes from being a woman.
Whenever I do anything
unfeminine,
I lose my laugh.

Norman Mailer
Author and frequent visitor

Chicago is the great American city,
   New York is one of the capitals of the world,
      and Los Angeles is a constellation of plastic;
   San Francisco is a lady. . . .

~~~~~~~

Dr. Marcus Conant
*At San Francisco author Randy Shilts's
memorial service following his death
from AIDS in 1994*

Randy had an incredible ability
to give speech to the agony in
gay America. He was both the
voice of gay America and the
conscience of straight America.

~~~~~~~

William Saroyan
Author and part-time San Francisco resident

It's an unreasonable city. It makes friends
of thieves . . . and opens its hearts to saints.
But only for a moment. It soon returns to
the thieves and abandons the saints.
It loves the good as well
as the evil.

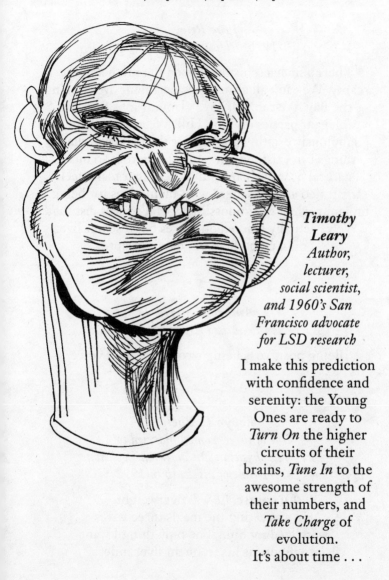

Timothy Leary
Author, lecturer, social scientist, and 1960's San Francisco advocate for LSD research

I make this prediction with confidence and serenity: the Young Ones are ready to *Turn On* the higher circuits of their brains, *Tune In* to the awesome strength of their numbers, and *Take Charge* of evolution.
It's about time . . .

Jane Riley
1970s television producer

There's such a schism between the myth and the reality. We can't all afford the apartment overlooking the Bay. We can't all have glamour jobs or go to elegant parties on Nob Hill. We can't all have fabulously exciting affairs. For the majority, these things can exist only in fantasy. There is so much natural beauty all around us here that many feel frustrated and impatient with themselves for being unhappy when the impossible dream proves just that. We've actually blamed ourselves because our lives didn't match an old movie script.

~~~~~~~

Ambrose Bierce
Early San Francisco Examiner columnist

Being positive is being wrong in a loud voice.

~~~~~~~

Robyn L. Phelps
One of three women married to
Bay Area physician Dr. Norman Lewiston
at the time of his death in 1992

Of course, he was overweight.
He was eating the meals three wives
were feeding him. The only thing I want
to inherit is his frequent flyer miles.

Alice Walker
San Francisco's most acclaimed novelist

I really do think that the men [in San Francisco] . . .
tend to be a lot more mellow here. Not as caught up in
the macho sensibility. They seem to relax
when they get here.

~~~~~~~~~

Anonymous single secretary
In the Financial District

San Francisco is a great town to eat in and
get drunk in, but it's not so great for single women.
I find all my boyfriends in the suburbs.

~~~~~~~~~

Ray Senhaux
Concierge at the Fairmont Hotel

There were these real nice guys from
Stockton, and one of them wanted to go
[to the Exotic Erotic ball] as a woman.
So I went down to Macy's and got him
a brassiere; basic black, of course.
As long as it's not illegal or immoral,
I'll do it. The saleslady asked,
"What size?" And I said, "Well,
he's about six-foot-three,
weighs about 210. . . ."

Herbert Gold
Writer

A walking town, blessedly limited
and cleansed by the bay and ocean,
San Francisco is also America's
last great metropolitan village.
It is a place to be explained,
like a blind man defining an
elephant—different wherever
you happen to touch it.

~~~~~~~

On a plaque
Behind California House Speaker
Willie Brown's desk

Old age and treachery
will overcome youth and skill.

~~~~~~~

The Los Angeles Herald Express
On the marriage of Joe DiMaggio
and Marilyn Monroe
at San Francisco City Hall

It could only happen here in America,
this storybook romance. . . .
Both of them had to fight their way
to fame and fortune and to each other,
one in a birthday suit and the other in a baseball suit.

Rob Morse
San Francisco Examiner columnist

San Franciscans don't have to worry about their city being called "Frisco" anymore. Everyone except flight attendants (who call it "San Fran") calls San Francisco "Sanfer Sisko." But, please, don't call it "Sisko."

~~~~~~~

Bill Mandel
San Francisco Examiner columnist, in 1979

Someone shot down a tourist from London on a cable car. Just shot him for no reason. But the man was taken care of so well in the hospital, people were so kind to him . . . he was quoted saying, "If you've got to be shot, San Francisco is the best place to be shot in."

M. F. K. Fisher
Food writer
and frequent
San Francisco visitor

San Francisco
 has been my
  family's escape
   hatch for . . .
    years,
     our favorite
       prescription
      for everything
      from blues to
    blahs to
   plain
  animal
   bliss.

CHAPTER 19

The Fog Rolls In

Jerry Dashkin
A visitor to San Francisco

A city of no seasons
but that of wet,
wind, and cold.

David Hulburd
In the San Francisco Chronicle

Ours is the finest fog in the United States.
Coming as it does right off the ocean,
it is clean, fresh fog, free from man-made
impurities. Our sunshine, which is the same
as sunshine anyplace, causes all our houses
to look white late in the afternoon.

Mark Twain
Writer and onetime
San Francisco resident

Behold, the same gust of wind
that blows a lady's dress aside
and exposes her ankle, fills your
eyes so full of sand that
you can't see it.

~~~~~~~~

Charles Groves
A visitor to San Francisco

A city with eleven months of winter
and several odd days of Indian Summer.

~~~~~~~~

Harold Gilliam
Nature writer

More than any other American
metropolis, San Francisco is a
city of the sea. . . . In San Francisco
not only are the ships of the world
visible from its hills; the currents
of the ocean and bay flow past it
on three sides; the salt winds and fogs
sweep through its streets;
the long Pacific combers perennially
pound its western boundary.

Herb Caen
San Francisco Chronicle columnist

I could see the fog venturing in like an unwelcome guest. First, with an apologetic shrug, it wraps its mantle around Alcatraz, as though to say: "Well, you won't miss seeing *this*, anyway." Soon it is drawn irresistibly to the whiteness of Coit Tower, first toying daintily with it, then suddenly gobbling it whole before your very eyes. Nurtured by this solid meal, the fog lunges at the Golden Gateway complex, obliterating its mass with obvious relish, and then slides into the bay, slithering onto the bridge and gobbling its succulent orange lights one by one. Then, fatter than a well-fed python, our monster from the sea settles down to sleep, and the city must sleep with it.